Sparks & Shards

Tiffany Leong

BookLeaf Publishing

India | USA | UK

Presentation by *BookLeaf Publishing*

Web: www.bookleafpub.com

E-mail: info@bookleafpub.com

ISBN : 9789358360332

First edition 2022

PREFACE

I have always been drawn to poems. Succinct and eloquently expressed, a simple prose can resonate with me for days. It's as if those couple of lines were specifically written for me.

Such poems inspired me to create my own. So I did. For my first compilation, I chose a theme that is always constant.

Love.

A short word that can transpire into precious memories, other emotions, and even self growth.

Here are a selected few, focusing solely on the love between two people.

I hope you enjoy reading these poems as much as I did in writing them.

With love,

Tiffany Leong

For those who have loved and lost,

you will love again

THE SEED

His eyes paint invisible paths on my face

Where his gaze lingers, my skin burns

A rose blossoms on my cheeks

And branches out towards my heart

His hands glide through the air

As his mouth formulates words

His baritone raises goosebumps

And shivers run down my spine

My breath hitches when he leans in

Sparks tingle at my fingertips

I yearn to close the gap

And press my lips against his

His smile is radiant and inviting

Like the gentle glow of sunshine

An illumination on fertile soils

Is this a seed of love?

SEE SAW

I miss the:

Interlaced fingers on casual strolls

Stolen kisses when no-one is looking

Whispered promises at the dusk of dawn

Tender comforts of unconditional support

Elusive journey to the forever after

I forget the:

Calendar clashes of balancing schedules

Random squabbles over anything and everything

Insecure tensions when there is silence

Constrained times left for family and friends

Loss of independence that comes with oneself

THE MESSAGES YOU LEFT ME

To the one who was emotionally unavailable:

I'm not the one who broke your heart.

To the one who wanted to remain friends:

How can you be a friend when you couldn't be a partner?

To the one who submarined seasonally:

I won't settle as your fallback choice.

To the one who was already taken:

Your partner is lucky to call you theirs.

To the one who was my polar opposite:

Thank you for showing me how the other half lives.

To the one who inspired proses:

A part of me will always love you.

To the one who was perfect while I healed:

You're the reason why I want to love again.

To me, cautious of more heartbreak:

You're yet to meet the one.

OUR SAGA

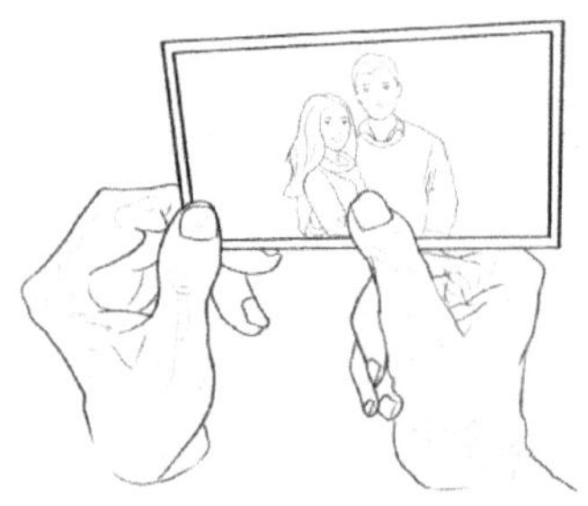

When we first met

You courted me perfectly

How could I forget

Since we lived in harmony

Once we were no longer nascent

I too reflected within

Had I become complacent

Over all that we had been?

But as time carried on

Days, months, and years

Happy moments were foregone

And I drowned in constant tears

So here we are today

Different times, different people

Going our separate ways

To the end, without a sequel

(UN)spoken words

Your smile is coy

Your fingers linger

Your voice is husky

As your eyes shimmer

You hold me closer

You whisper me delights

You say there's no-one finer

As you turn off the lights

I soak in your praises

Relish in your touch

I am lost in a daze

And I tighten my clutch

Yet all these are just a proxy

Of what I truly want to hear

Perhaps one day you'll decree:

I love you too, my dear

YOU, ME, ANEW

A chance encounter

With a familiar stranger

Hair, same shade

But in a braid

Eyes, brilliant blue

But warmth subdued

You saunter nearer

My heartbeats quiver

I swallow my dread

To clear my head

Our gazes meet

But it's bittersweet

Nothing yet spoken

Before scars reopen

My heart broke before

And it will once more

For now I finally see

You and me will never be

BLACK GRAVITY

Atramentous

Electrifying

Indulgent

They were the feelings

When our eyes locked

Breathless

Frozen

Gooseflesh

They were the effects

When your gaze remained

Awestruck

Besotted

Intrigued

They were the thoughts

When I continued to walk

Wistful

Serene

Elation

They were the hopes

When I wandered on

EMINENCE

Tresses of coppery gold

A pearly complexion that glows

Emerald eyes glitter with mischief

Above a splatter of bronze specks

A hint of rose on the cheeks

Finished with ruby lips in a smile

I finally met the royal treasure

MINH AND JULIAN

Outside their intimate bubble

Those who sit nearby

Scrutinise the connection

To sense their level of affection

Minh - pale with black hair

Eyes the colour of espresso

Julian - tanned with golden locks

Eyes the shade of deep cobalt

Polar opposites, aesthetically

Yet they sit rather close

They divide and share a croissant

And stir coffee like an enfant

Discuss their commonalities

Careers and studies in health

Love of travel, country hopping

Every explanation in ESL

Minh yearns for more than friends

His eyes trail after every move

His barest touch lingers too long

His true dream for a love returned

Julian now has an Oceania contact

A link for his medical vocation

Another foreigner for him to guide

To fulfil his quest for inner pride

They soon take their last sip

Dust off the buttery crumbs

Wave over the junior waiter

And stand up for departure

Julian is completely inspired

Energised for the rest of the day

Minh is about to blether

In hopes that one day

They'll leave together

NUMB

It feels as though

A dagger's wedged in the heart

Surrounded by broken shards

Twisted deep and forever buried

So that it will never, ever heal

The tears no longer flow

Migraines in lieu of stomach aches

But the breaths come out in gasps

Followed by longing, raspy wails

For rationale in the nonsense

When the pain becomes overwhelming

Pop a pill and kill the mood

Everything is then nothing

The mind stops racing

And all the worries melt away

Behind closed eyes and in muted dreams

Flashbacks of an iridescent pair

Sunshines and butterflies before the storm

The reach of a rainbow so elusive

Unless the tablets are relinquished

LIGHTS

I only saw the green

Handsome stranger

Polite guest

Proud homeowner

Family stalwart

Adventure seeker

Experimental cook

Frequent traveller

Casual athlete

Young entrepreneur

And ignored the amber

Question avoider

Abrupt texter

Stingy spender

Purposeful forgetter

Dates rescheduler

Charming womaniser

Pompous humblebragger

Until they all turned red

Constant workaholic

Friendless recluse

Manipulative sycophant

Conniving masochist

Tyrannical gasligher

FICTION ROMANCE

I fell in love before I knew love

Relished in words on page

Identified with protagonists in movies

Fantasised the perfect partner

All traits from TV Tropes

Tall, Dark, and Handsome

Made of Iron

Byronic Hero

Perhaps if I had immersed differently

I'd pine for a different character

Someone who didn't need saving

As he was complete all along

FROM THIS DAY FORWARD...

In sickness and in health

These vows were exchanged

Shrouded in an abundance of wealth

I never thought we'd be estranged

Flash forward a couple of years

An accident, multiple scars

Every shadow heightened your fears

And our room was littered with cigars

I was then blamed for your despair

Your kindness morphed into cruelty

You'd glower, scream, and yank my hair

So I yielded to your insanity

I yearned to escape this daily nightmare

But I recalled the pledge from the heart

Whispered in a fervent prayer:

Until death do us part...

FIVE LANGUAGES OF LOVE

Words of Affirmation

'You can do anything.'

'You look ravishing.'

'You make me happy.'

'I love you.'

Quality Time

A private dinner

Joint activities

Thoughtful discussions

Incessantly undivided attention

Acts of Service

Handling household chores

Baking favourite treats

Running the tiresome errands

Actions without being asked

Physical Touch

A greeting kiss

Warm embrace

Interlaced hands

Always an absentminded caress

Receiving Gifts

Birthdays, anniversaries, occasions

A randomly plucked flower

Personally handcrafted mementos

Any item that reminded you of me

1, 2, 3, 4, 5

You do them all

BINARY

I rose at dawn with a peaceful smile

You slept past midnight with a yawn

I licked chocolate off the spoons

You picked at my leftover chips

I composed new songs on the piano

You engaged in new active sports

I arrived on time to all my commitments

You sauntered in often several minutes late

I relaxed in solitude

You delighted in gatherings

I frolicked in nature

You strolled through cities

I followed my heart

You followed your head

We agreed to disagree

And finished at goodbye

FAIRY TALE

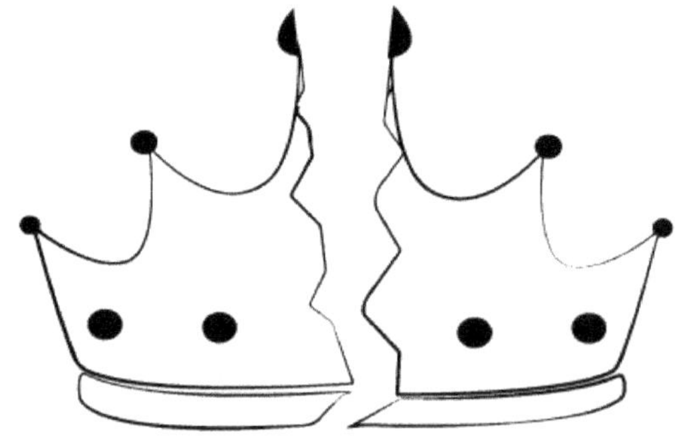

Once upon a time, in a land far away

There was an orphan who slept on hay

She befriended all the forest creatures

Who became her trusted, lifelong teachers

She grew up beautiful, kind, and humble

From all that she built, made from rubble

One day while she was having a rinse

She caught the eye of the kingdom's prince

For him, it was love at first sight

And he declared they'd wed that very night

The girl wept goodbye to all her friends

Promising she'd return to make amends

She was whisked away to the grand castle

Where she never had to lift another muscle

But when she saw the servants' duties

She couldn't stand being an idle beauty

She took upon herself the mansion's chores

Sweeping and scrubbing the marble floors

When the prince saw that she behaved as a
maid

He demanded she stop her shameful
charade

So the girl abdicated her royal position

No longer yielding to his cruel submission

She eagerly left for her home by the prairie

Where all along, she had been merry

JUST TWO FRIENDS

Everyone wonders if there's something more

Between the two friends who live next door

The pair are often lost in their private bubble

Where she will giggle and he will chuckle

Amidst the rowdy crowds of their mates

They bemoan about their dreadful dates

Still, no-one ever sees the two of them flirt

Though sometimes they don the other's shirt

Yet when they're alone, her heartbeats flutter

At the gentlest touch, she melts like butter

She longs for an epic romance to occur

I know all this, because I am her

BY/GONE

I miss you

I've pined for others before

But never on this degree of anguish

A gaping void

Where you stoically nourished it with love

You were always there without being there

I can't focus

You haunt all my waking moments

Nightmares too, as dreams of you aren't true

Nothing means anything

They're either reminiscent of past times

Or new memories created without you

I will persevere

Remember who I was before we met

Heal and evolve into a better me

Before the pain dissipates

It affirms our connection was real

So I cling on before its eventual end

IN/DEPENDENCE

Right from the start

We'd never been apart

From our first rendezvous

I knew that I'd fall for you

Not a day went by

Without you saying hi

After many exuberant dates

I deemed us soulmates

I never felt smothered

But always treasured

You provided unwavering support

No matter who or what was at fault

As you'd be my last suitor

You were part of my future

Our family and friends intertwined

While our new priorities were aligned

Then we started to unravel

From a multitude of sharp cavils

Simultaneously, we'll both move on

But this time, we'll do it on our own

RECALIBRATE

Alarm pings jolt up dash out the door. Yoga work gym cook read walk dog TV if there's time. Family friends some nights same on weekends add extended events conferences parties hobbies. Calendar full book in advance. Nothing new but satisfied.

Then you.

Drift in with a smile you encircle. Covertly always present until you're in the schedule. Encourage patience priorities passions.

Trigger forgotten emotions. Giddiness adrenaline desire.

Things slow.

Happier.

ACKNOWLEDGEMENTS

I would like to thank my family, the first people to show me unconditional love.

Thank you to all my friends who have laughed and cried with me. In this journey, we spoke about the romantic escapades until they took flight in written form.

Finally, thanks to all the partners, past, present, and future. You taught me that emotions can form some beautiful pieces of work.